A STUDIO PRESS BOOK

First published in the UK in 2020 by Studio Press,
an imprint of Bonnier Books UK,
The Plaza, 535 King's Road, London SW10 0SZ

www.studiopressbooks.co.uk
www.bonnierbooks.co.uk

1 3 5 7 9 10 8 6 4 2

ISBN 978-1-78741-613-0

Written by Milly Smith
Illustrated by Katie Abey
Edited by Frankie Jones
Designed by Rob Ward

A CIP catalogue for this book is available from the British Library
Printed and bound in China

Dedicated to my best friend and husband, Rishi Bhaskara.

- Milly Smith

To Jeff, for inspiring me and for helping me
to attempt to adult every day.

- Katie Abey

CONTENTS

CONTENTS

INTRODUCTION

You know those things that you're supposed to know how to do as an adult, but you really don't know?

Things like making small talk in a hairdresser's or going clothes shopping without having a breakdown?

You know those moments that everyone around you seems to sail through whilst you're left splashing around in the water?

Like feeling pride in your achievements, making plans you know you're actually going to stick to and being gentle on yourself?

You know those nights you spend alone in your own mind whilst it seems like everyone else is living their best life?

Do you find yourself scrolling an endless sea of perfected photos whilst you wallow in darkness with stains down your hoodie?

There's adulting and then there's adulting for the messy mind. Basic adulting for the bumbling brain if you will.

Sound familiar?

Don't worry, you're in the right place.

WE GOT YOU

So, how do you even use an adulting manual?

It's quite simple! Follow these steps on how you can use your adulting manual to its full potential.

Step 1:
Use the manual as much or as little as you need.

Step 2:
Be messy, be neat, dampen the book with tears or roll your eyes at the terrible jokes... it doesn't matter. Use it in your own way.

Step 3:
Repeat steps 1 and 2.

This is your safe space, do with it what you will; I'm not judging (I promise).

If you get a bit stuck on how to let your thoughts and creativity flow, try picking up your manual when you feel anger, intense sadness, low moods or even when you feel nothing at all.

Pop the book in your bag, hide it under your pillow or whack it on your desk at work.

Keep it with you for any time you need a release.

I'm here for ya!

5

Who do you think you are?

I like to be called: _ _ _ _ _ _ _ _ _ _ _ _ _ _ _ _ _ _

I identify as: _

My pronouns are: _ _ _ _ _ _ _ _ _ _ _ _ _ _ _ _ _ _

I've lived on this planet _ _ _ _ _ _ years.

I'm pretty rad because: _ _ _ _ _ _ _ _ _ _ _
_ _

It's okay if you can't think of anything right now, revisit this page another time.

We can't always appreciate our rad-ness.

Use this space to doodle or write the important things in your life.

You could scribble about your pals, your favourite t-shirt, food you enjoy or perhaps a few lyrics of your most loved song.

What do you want from this manual?

(I'm sorry to say it can't grant you three wishes.)

Write what you hope to achieve or work on whilst using this book.

Maybe you're training for a marathon or you might just want to work on making sure you have a daily shower.

ˈIt doesn't matter what it is, working on yourself isn't a competition.

I want to work on: _____

_____

_____

I want to achieve: _____

_____

_____

Body image, body acceptance and body love

Welcome to the first chapter, here you will find ways to combat and break down beauty standards, challenge your own negative inner voice and (hopefully) start to make friends with your body.

Turn the page and begin to unlearn everything you've been told about beauty, raise your self-worth and stamp on those body worries.

You are NOT your body

Believe it or not, your walking, fleshy prison isn't the best or the worst thing about you.

I am more than this!

We all feel it.

You're not alone if you feel that your worth is directly linked to your waist size, but it doesn't stop it from being utter BS.

We are bombarded from kiddyhood with diet imagery showing 'happiness' found in lb lost and perpetually told one body type is 'in' whilst our body shape is totally 'out'.

It seems no one is left unscathed.

Colour us in!

Decorate me

Think of your body as a cake box.

The box is there to transport and protect the contents and whilst it holds a job of great importance (gotta protect that cake!), it's the goodness inside that really matters.

It's the soul feeding, fulfilling sweetness that lies within that truly makes you, you.

Don't let your transporting box determine the beauty within.

We're going to explore what makes you, **you**!

Write a few notes about yourself that don't include your appearance. They can be positive or neutral (try to avoid putting yourself down). Think of things that make you who you are. Imagine everyone could only see your personality instead of your body.

What would people see?

I've started you off with a little prompt, hope it helps!

When I think of myself, I think of: _____

_____

_____

Sometimes I can be: _____

_____

_____

My qualities include: _____

_____

_____

It's okay...

It's okay if all that comes to mind is negativity, if that is the case then revisit this page when you've learnt how awesome you really are OR write down wonderful things others have said about you!

Isn't it straight up crap how each of us are so amazingly different in our own unique way but only a teeny tiny amount of us are actually represented in the media? **Not cool.**

Diversity is not only beautiful, but it just is. It's life.

Instead of shaming the wonderful diversity around us and shying away from it, let's celebrate it, embrace it and just simply accept it.

My scars don't define me.

I am a valid male.

Worthy of respect.

Draw your amazing self here and join this bloomin' beautiful lot.

What would your inspirational mantra be?

Mirror, mirror on the changing room wall

Picture this: you, centre stage, spotlights shining on your half-naked body in front of the most judgmental audience waiting for you to squeeze your way into mannequin-shaped clothing.

What a thrill ride, huh?

Let's face it: clothes shopping can be traumatising, but it doesn't have to be that way! With a little understanding and self-acceptance we can stop the cycle of body woes in changing rooms.

You are not shaped like this.

It's **NOT** your body that's the issue. High-street clothing is made to fit to a very limited body shape and size and is designed for those who are able-bodied. It's pretty shit that the majority of stores aren't celebrating our unique and wonderful population. Remember, the shame lies with them, not with you and your glorious fleshy frame.

Forget the trends, forget what size is on the label (clothes sizing is horrifically inconsistent) and forget what you feel you **SHOULD** be dressing in.

Wear what makes **YOU** feel like **YOU!**

If clothing woes weren't weighing you down what would your dream outfit be?

Design it or describe it here and work towards getting your fine self in it for real. You deserve to express yourself and **OWN IT!**

Top tips for your next shopping trip

Try out these tips and hints to make your shopping experience a little easier and leave a little tick if it worked! ✓

☐ **It's okay to leave**

Ultimately, you want to avoid a meltdown. If you start to feel like you can't quell those nasty voices, then leave! Forget how cute the jeans are... they're not worth jeopardising your mental health.

☐ **Psyche yourself up**

Use positive and gentle affirmations:

My body is fine the way it is.

Thoughts aren't fact.

I'm not going to let this crumble me today.

It's not worth my happiness.

I ain't worth it.

☐ **No surprises**

Become acquainted with your body. Strip down and quite literally lay it bare, trace your body with your eyes or hands and learn every lump, curve and roll.

☐ **Be ignorant AF**

Don't waltz in to the store throwing dagger eyes at everyone who dares to look at you, but do put up your metaphorical blinkers. Focus on yourself and your own needs. Breathe, put some music on and relax.

☐ **Privacy please**

If a store offers returns, then simply take the clothes home to try on. Familiar surroundings and privacy can be comforting and will help to hush any negative inner talk so you can try the items on and see that you totally rock them.

☐ **Size it**

Check and research which shops have a range of clothing to suit your body. Support the stores that cater to all of us and avoid the shops you know will trigger you.

15

Comparing isn't cool

Cinematic masterpieces are flawless for a reason: we only see the final cut.

The bloopers and mistakes are removed. Use this metaphor when thinking about social media, we are seeing the 'cinematic' version of a life and the blooper reel is hidden.

Make peace with the idea that perfection is unattainable. Take it off your mood-board, swipe it out of your vocabulary and revel in your imperfect highs and lows. Ride the waves and experience the thrill.

Comparing your own movie to someone else's story will only lead to disappointment and low self-esteem.

Calm seas never make for a skilled surfer!

What would the title of your life movie be?

Celebrating our own achievements without comparison is mega important.

Don't forget that celebrating the achievements of others without comparing them to anyone else is also up there on the mega important scale.

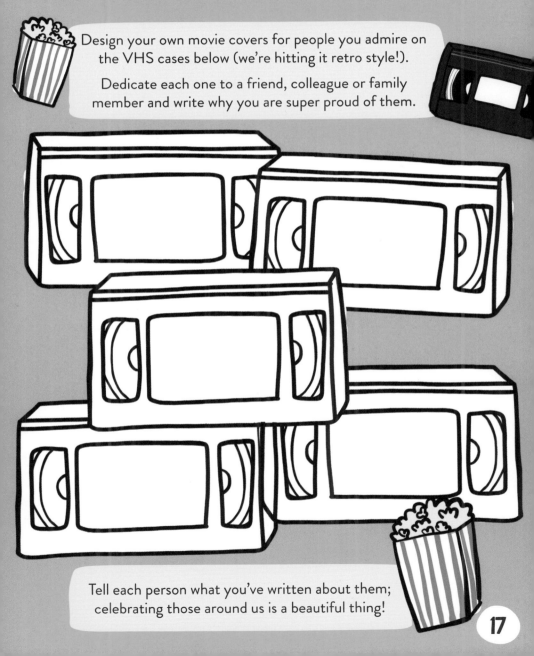

Design your own movie covers for people you admire on the VHS cases below (we're hitting it retro style!).

Dedicate each one to a friend, colleague or family member and write why you are super proud of them.

Tell each person what you've written about them; celebrating those around us is a beautiful thing!

Embrace it

A hug does absolute wonders for our brain juices and it's okay to give yourself a big ol' squeeze, a quick soft touch or a relaxing head scratch.

Skin to skin is not only grounding but calming and centring!

Stroke your face gently.

Trace the veins on your arms.

ACTIVITY TIME!

Touch yourself!

Seriously, embrace the hell out of yourself.

Gently squeeze your hands together.

Massage your scalp.

Hug yourself (sure you may look a tad weird but who cares?!).

Getting to know your body can help you avoid avoiding it.

It's also super relaxing and helps with the release of serotonin (the happy chemical). Do it in a traffic jam, when work is stressing you out or just at home in front of the TV.

Colour me!

My body does NOT define me

19

Ditch the diets

Oh hi, just dropping in to let you know that around 95% of diets don't work... seriously, don't blame yourself.

A quick show of hands if you've been on a few diets already? Is your hand raised?

Well I guarantee you're not alone (my hand is up there too).

Ever heard the term 'I'm having a health-kick' thrown around, when what they really mean is they're flying off to Diet Island (formally known as Soul Sucking Resort)?

Anti-diet isn't anti-healthy eating; they're not synonymous!

Diet culture thrives on feeding lies (excuse the pun).

The diet industry is a business that runs on profit **NOT** happiness and health.

With diets comes restrictions which digs up cravings.

Unfed cravings can lead us to obsess over and binge on the very food we're trying to avoid.

Can you guess what might follow on from that? Yep, guilt.

Guilt for listening to what our body naturally wants.

Stick the 'Contains food NOT guilt' sticker from the back of your manual on to your fridge!

Intuitive eating
AKA natural eating habits

If you want to see intuitive eating in full swing simply watch a toddler eat.

They experience pleasure in their food, feel no guilt and subconsciously respect their body's cues.

Unfortunately, intuitive eating is something that no longer comes naturally to many of us, so below are some tips on how to get back into your body's natural rhythm and kick diet culture to the curb.
Who's with me?

Honour your hunger

It's okay to be hungry even after you just ate. Honour it. Your body is a smarty pants, it knows what it needs.

Question it

Have I had too much?
Do I really want this?
Get in tune with your body, it'll answer your questions!

Guilt be gone

Food is never 'naughty' and you're not 'naughty' for eating more or less. Enjoy the food. You're allowed to.

Respect your meal times

I know life is busy but try and take a moment out of the day to enjoy your food in peace. Really pay attention to every mouthful.

Count smiles not calories

Calorie counting is detrimental and unhelpful. You have your own calorie and nutrition counter right inside you so use it and listen to your body.

What foods do you avoid due to diet culture?
If you can, try to enjoy some of these soon!

Body image boosters

Here are some amazing ways to help you boost your body image.

Scribble down ways to incorporate these boosters into your every day routine* – and then try them out! Add your own ideas, too.

Write

Grab some skin-friendly pens or make-up pencils and write positive wording all over your body parts.

Draw flowers, scribble pretty patterns and decorate yourself!

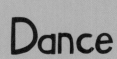

Dance

Move however your body permits you to. Feel and enjoy every jiggle. Even basic movements and rhythm keeping is dancing!

Sing

Make up your own lyrics or scream your favourite feel-good song **AT THE TOP OF YOUR LUNGS** for maximum effect.

Compliment

Say kind things to yourself AND others! Get into the habit of giving yourself and those around you little compliments.

Exercise

Exercise does not have to be regimented and strict!

Move in a way that makes you feel awesome and gets some endorphins flowing.

A nice walk in the sun, a stretch in your wheelchair or a cross-fit class with pals, it's up to you!

* I say this loosely because do any of us actually have a proper adult routine?

Mental
health

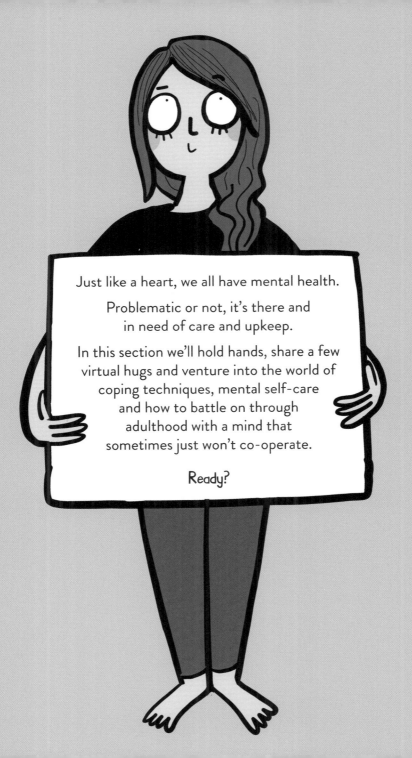

Thoughts aren't fact

We have over 60,000 thoughts a day.
That's a lot of times we are potentially self-sabotaging and bullying ourselves. It sucks, but negative thoughts are going to creep in, and we can't banish that fully, but we can take a step back to question the pesky thoughts and try to apply some logic.

Thinking something does **NOT** make it fact, so why do we react to our negative thoughts as though they are the truth. Thoughts can be hazy and float in and out so let them.

We don't need to cross examine every thought like your best friend looking through your love interest's Facebook page.

Let's crack on with a little exercise.

Don't worry, you can keep your butt parked where it is, I just need your mind.

What thoughts are plaguing your mind you right now?

Write them down (if you've got an overflowing worry-worm mind I advise a spare sheet of paper) and for each thought answer these three questions:

Thought one: _____

_____

Thought two: _____

_____

Is this a fact?

Remember, you having a fleeting thought doesn't automatically make it fact.

Your assumptions aren't fact either.

Thought one: _____

Thought two: _____

Is it fuelled by something else?

Perhaps by anxiety, a low mood or external pressures. This might help you find the reason behind the thoughts, giving yourself understanding and insight.

Thought one: _____

Thought two: _____

What can I do to challenge these thoughts?

Get a little sassy with those thoughts and throw some facts at them.

You could challenge the thought of feeling useless with a counteracting thought: I cracked on with a day even when my low mood felt impossibly hard.

Thought one: _____

_____

_____

Thought two: _____

_____

_____

It may help to revisit this page when you feel troubling thoughts creeping in.

27

Cry me a river
— no really, you're allowed

You're allowed to cry.

Batman cries (maybe... I'd like to think he does. He deals with a lot.)

Don't let anyone invalidate you because of your tears. They are not a sign of weakness or incapacity.

I cry because...

...and that's ok

Crying is healthy and cleansing for your mind and soul.

Crying is a normal emotion. Some people don't cry and some of us cry at everything from koalas in woolly jumpers to grief and loss.

I cry because...

...and that's ok

I cry because...

...and that's ok

Crying doesn't mean you're:

- Oversensitive
- Overreacting
- Just hormonal
- Weak
- Being irrational
- Not a total badass

Change of plans

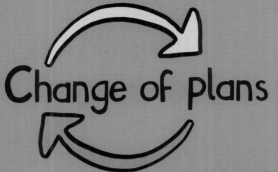

Sorry I can't make it

Guilt is a common emotion that is associated with a messy adult mind.

Have you ever felt guilt for something insignificant, like cancelling a coffee date or not texting someone back for a few days?

Here are some text ideas to make it a little easier on your mind for when you do need to cancel plans. Try them out and add a few of your own.

Sending that gut-wrenching message of 'Hey, I'm going to have to cancel again' can leave you feeling useless and guilty.

You're not any of these things.

You're human and it's okay to need to cancel.

Hiya, can we skip today? I'm not feeling great and I want to honour it by not pushing myself too far.

Hello, today is a grey day for me. I need to look after myself at home but let's reschedule.

Hey, my mind is a mess today, let's revisit when I'll be able to give you my full attention.

Have you remembered to take your meds?

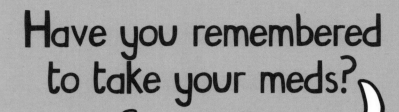

FOR SHAME

EASY WAY OUT

WEAK

CHEMICAL NONSENSE

These phrases may sound familiar if you take medication for your mental health. Perhaps remarks like these have even stopped you from considering taking medication in the first place.

Shame around medication is still common and is brutally relentless.

Whether it's a lack of education surrounding the topic or the ever present stigma around mental health, this shame is dehumanising and discriminatory.

It's hard to see past the shaming and negative views, so let me help. Here's a visual explanation:

Think of your mental health as the flatpack bookcase and the tools as mental health medication. The man-made serotonin may give you the appropriate tools, but you still have to do the building. Taking medication is **NOT** the easy way out: it's giving those without the natural tools a chance at building the flatpack.

Meds or no meds, you're a badass!

Have you considered medication but felt too plagued with shame?

Write a list of the things that have stopped you from seeking help in tablet form:

Taking medication for your mental health does not make you a failure; it actually requires a lot of strength to acknowledge you need the help and to then seek it out.

Badass 10mg

Yassss 5g

Strong AF 200mcg

150mcg
Not weak

You're the best 30mg

POP THE STICKER HERE

Are any of these things more important than your mental health?*

Go on, make the call to your GP and give yourself a scary phone call sticker from the back of the manual. Proud of you.

*Remember, your mental health comes first so I guess I've answered that for you. Oops!

Not diarrhoea but depression

We rarely feel remorse when ringing into work with a hangover, claiming horrific illness (we've all done it), however ringing in to say we are genuinely poorly with our mental health fills us with leg-shaking anxiety, nervous sweats and reluctancy often so strong that we don't do it.

Here are some ways you can ring in sick for mental health (yes, you're allowed):

Hello, I'm sorry I won't be making it in today as I am unwell.

I'm worried that my mental health will affect my job today. It's safer for me to take this day to collect my mind so I will be taking this day as sick.

Hello, I won't be making it into work today as I am struggling with my mental health. I will be taking today as a sick day, sorry for the inconvenience.

Right, pull out your drama skills because it's time for some amdram.

I want you to pick up your phone and pretend to ring in sick for your mental health.

Go on, no one's judging you, and it could potentially be helpful if you ever need to do it for real.

How did it go?
Write a few notes in as prompts.

Keep going

It's not often I encourage digging up bad memories but occasionally you'll find that buried alongside a bad memory are little shards of strength and pride that haven't yet seen the light of day.

It can't hurt you.

Firstly, I want you to check yourself; are you in a strong mindset?

Are you okay with thinking of past hard times? If not, skip this page and revisit it when you feel ready.

Grab some paper and a pen, remember that whatever you write on this paper can be ripped up and thrown away in an instant.

Take a deep breath and write one bad memory in the middle of the paper.

Perhaps a night that felt impossible to carry on from or a memory that you thought would stop you in your tracks forever.

Now surround this memory with ways that you kept going and how you survived.

I made it to the sunrise

I carried on fighting, it didn't beat me

Feel pride.

Feel a sense of strength.

Realise you CAN beat those dark nights.

Repeat this activity as much as needed.

I am allowed to...

Adults fuck up. Adults make small, medium and **COLLOSAL** mistakes. Adults aren't perfect. You aren't perfect. Stop expecting yourself to be.

You're allowed to mess up; you're a human! Adulthood is about making mistakes, owning them, accepting them and learning from them. Perfect is a myth, so allow yourself a chance to grow and bloom.

Don't hide yourself away in shame.

I am allowed to feel like shit.

I am allowed to binge animated films snuggled under my favourite blanket.

I am allowed to...

I am allowed to...

On these pages, write things that you are **ALLOWED** to do (yep, even as super responsible adults doing adulty things).

I am allowed to still snooze with my childhood bear.

I am allowed to...

I am allowed to...

I am allowed to...

I am allowed to...

35

Why me?

It's 9 p.m. and you're lying on the kitchen floor after yet another ungodly breakdown. You're not sure how you're going to make it into work tomorrow, you're waiting for the floor to eat you alive and your mind is swirling with angry thoughts of 'why me?'.

Anger and frustration caused by mental health problems is **NORMAL**.

Forget the world's tiniest violin playing the world's saddest song.

Feeling sorry for yourself and feeling anger is nothing to be ashamed of.

Smash that tiny violin, and why not blow this **HUGE** trumpet?

It sucks that anyone has to struggle through a messy mind.

Shout about it.

Blow the trumpet and let loose some of the pressure!

Write some of your anger along the sound waves or scribble and add to the noise coming out the trumpet! Be heard, even if just by yourself!

Counselling is cool

Going to therapy or counselling should be treated in the same way as going to the GP for a physical ailment.

It's just 'my brain needs some help!' instead of 'my back needs some help!'

Talking, screaming or even whispering about your feelings is helpful as fuck so let's reduce the stigma and allow our mind to seek help when it's calling out in pain!

Family/group therapy

Art therapy

Relationship therapy

Mindfulness/ meditation

Brief therapy

Online therapy

Coaching

Traditional therapy doesn't work for everyone.

Talking therapy might just make you want to vomit BUT fear not because therapy and counselling can come in many forms.

Colour or tick the therapies that spark an interest and when you're ready, take the step to search for something similar in your area.

What have you got to lose and what have you got to gain?

Art therapy

Multimodal therapy

Guidance counselling

Solution-focused therapy

Hypnotherapy

Search online and find what works for YOU!

What MY mental health feels like

Perception of mental health is different for everyone. Whilst the images on the previous page may relate to some, they may seem completely wrong for you and that's perfectly okay.

So, what does YOUR mental health feel like?

Draw or write about it below.

Draw one thing or draw 10, fill the page or leave it empty.
This is your space.

prove
them
wrong

Hydrate

By adulthood we're normally into the swing of keeping ourselves physically hydrated (coffee counts, right?), but are you emotionally hydrated?

Try a brain exercise app

Social media break

More time for hobbies

Don't answer emails past 6 p.m.

Maybe you've heard of the phrase 'you can't pour from an empty cup', so why are we forever letting ours run dry?

We're not much help to anyone, especially ourselves if we're not quenching our own emotional thirst sufficiently.

Fill this glass with refreshing, sloshing things you're going to do to hydrate your emotional state, whether that's doing sweet F-all or guarding your energy.

43

If three-year-olds get sticker rewards for visiting the dentist, then you best believe adults can too! Use the stickers from the back of your manual to place inside these medals and trophies when you've earnt them and congratulate your badass self for doing... things!

Riding the lows and coping with crisis

Helplines

Before you go any further please know this... it's okay to ask for help.

If it feels like there's no one to turn to on a dark night or you're at a loss as to what to do and you feel like all hope is lost then don't hesitate to pick up the phone; you'll hear someone on the other end who wants to help, and I think that's pretty damn incredible.

Feeling nervous is okay. These people are trained and are just happy and proud to hear your voice.

Here are some numbers which might be useful.

Anxiety UK
For those affected by anxiety disorders.
Call 03444 775 774
9.30 a.m.-5.30 p.m. Monday-Friday

Beat Eating Disorders
Support for individuals experiencing an eating disorder and their loved ones.
Call 0808 801 0677
12 p.m.-8 p.m. Monday-Friday and 4 p.m.-8 p.m. weekends and bank holidays

Mind
For better mental health.
Call 0300 123 3393
9 a.m.-6 p.m. Monday-Friday

National Domestic Abuse Freephone Helpline
Provides specialist services to survivors of domestic abuse.
Call 0808 2000 247
24 hours a day, 365 days a year
If you are in immediate danger, please call 999.

National Bullying Helpline
Information and advice for adults affected by bullying at work, or cyberbullying.
Call 0845 22 55 787
9 a.m.-5 p.m. Monday-Friday

No Panic
Help for people who suffer from panic attacks, phobias, OCD and other related anxiety disorders.
Call 0844 967 4848
10 a.m.-10 p.m., 7 days a week

Samaritans
For anyone having a difficult time.
Call 116 123
24 hours a day, 365 days a year

Switchboard
A safe space for the LGBT+ community.
0300 330 0630
10 a.m.-10 p.m., 7 days a week

Victim Support
Support for victims of crime
0808 1689 111
24 hours a day, 365 days a year

Crisis plan

Having a plan B is helpful but not if you don't even have a plan A!

Crisis plans serve the purpose of being your logical step-by-step when your mind might be working against you.

Practise on a piece of paper and write your final version here:

My crisis plan

My warning signs of a low mood are:

_____

_____

_____

If I start to feel low, I can distract myself by:

_____

_____

_____

If my distractions don't work, I can call/text:

_____

_____

_____

If they don't answer I can use a local crisis line which is:

_____

_____

_____

If I have an urge to hurt myself, I can go here to keep myself safe:

_____

_____

A lot of things aren't certain in adulthood but the rising and setting of the sun is for definite. Today will pass and a new dawn will break bringing with it a whole day of possibilities, new beginnings and hope.

Today, and whatever mood that's come along with it, will pass.

I have so much left to give.

I have new memories to make and smiles to have.

I can try the new gingerbread latte.

What have you got to look forward to after the dark times pass? Add your own ideas.

Gentle but powerful

You've heard of *less is more* but have you heard of *gentle is powerful*? Probably not because I just made it up.

During our hardest times we need to be kind to ourselves, so here are some super gentle phrases you can use instead of being a down right meanie to yourself (you can also use them with others when they're having a rough time too).

Flowers can't bloom all year.

I deserve a relaxing evening after a stressful day.

I am allowed to heal and move on from mistakes.

I am not responsible for the happiness of others.

There's always tomorrow.

I tried my best.

I am not going to rise to an argument, I am going to protect myself.

I had a rough day, I need some space and clarity, I deserve it.

I can't please everybody, that's not my job.

Each time you use one of these quotes with either yourself or a friend colour in a petal. Make these flowers bloom whilst making yourself bloom too!

It's not all bad

The world may feel all doom and gloom right now, but did you know that there's an animal called a **DIK-DIK**... Oh come on, that made you smile a little didn't it? If not, here are some totally ridiculous yet adorable facts to show you the world isn't always shit.

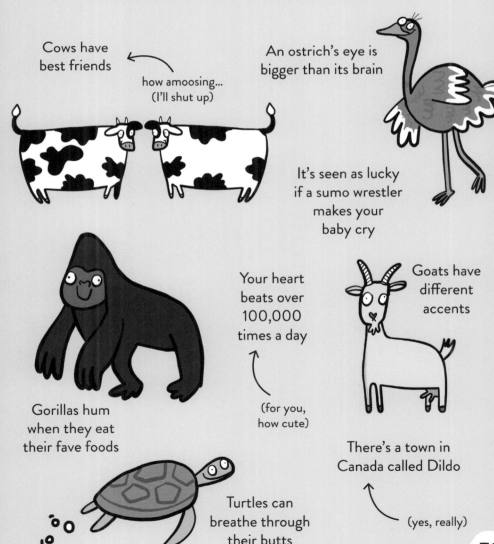

Cows have best friends

how amoosing...
(I'll shut up)

An ostrich's eye is bigger than its brain

It's seen as lucky if a sumo wrestler makes your baby cry

Your heart beats over 100,000 times a day

(for you, how cute)

Goats have different accents

Gorillas hum when they eat their fave foods

Turtles can breathe through their butts

There's a town in Canada called Dildo

(yes, really)

How to do... stuff

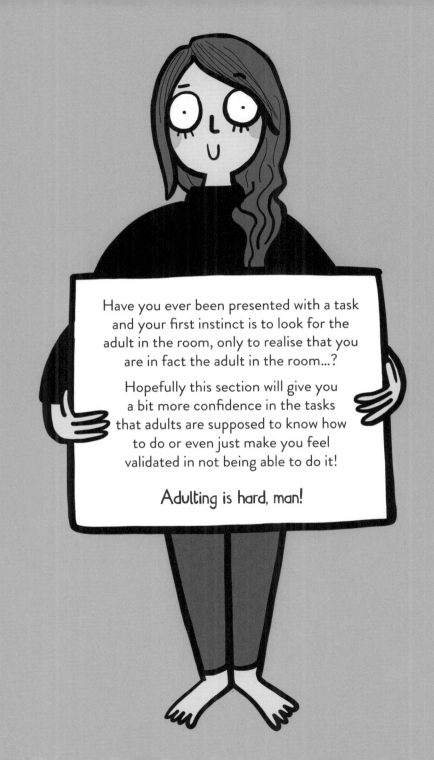

Have you ever been presented with a task and your first instinct is to look for the adult in the room, only to realise that you are in fact the adult in the room...?

Hopefully this section will give you a bit more confidence in the tasks that adults are supposed to know how to do or even just make you feel validated in not being able to do it!

Adulting is hard, man!

Small talk, big challenge

Get through any small talk situation with these simple prompts. Add your own and circle the ones that prove successful (you're welcome!).

Challenge

Talk

'Sorry, I need the toilet, I'll catch you later!'

Know how to end it
Look at your watch and politely say you've got somewhere to be, but it was lovely chatting. Remember that you are allowed to leave a situation whenever you like. Be polite but firm!

'Oh amazing, I bet you're proud.'

'Aw, so sweet.'

Prepare some generic responses
(You know... for times like when Tina the hairdresser is telling you the 100th story about her kids.)

'Ah wow, that's awesome.'

Don't be afraid to tell them!
A lot of factors can add to why you're anxious of small talk and you are allowed to tell people you don't wish to talk!

Having your hair done? Tell your hairdresser that you like it done without talking so you can relax, they'll be sure to comply!

Sat next to a chatterbox on the train? Let them know politely that you like to switch off or meditate on journeys.

'I see, what led you into that?'

'Oh really, how come?'

Make them do the talking!
If you're a better listener than you are small talker, be sneaky and ask more questions!

'Amazing, what does that entail?'

The universal sign for 'STFU, I don't wanna talk.'

How to sleep

I don't know about you, but I've been running on empty since day one. Who are these mythical people who have a healthy sleep cycle?

Well, with these tips it could be you!

 Switch it: Keep your house dimly lit 1-2 hours before bed time.

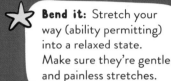 **Bend it:** Stretch your way (ability permitting) into a relaxed state. Make sure they're gentle and painless stretches.

 Dump it: Empty your mind before bed, don't sleep on a messy mind. Write a list of the top things bothering you each night. Move them from head to paper!

 Think it: Try guided meditation (search YouTube or Spotify).

 Plant it: Try herbal plant tea or an aromatherapy pillow spray. Plant power!

Weigh it: A weighted blanket helps ease anxiety and restless legs!

 Describe or draw your perfect sleepy space here and work towards making it a reality!

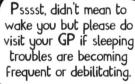 Psssst, didn't mean to wake you but please do visit your GP if sleeping troubles are becoming frequent or debilitating.

 Remember, there's no shame in seeking help!

Colour in these swear words

Fuck
Bollocks
shit
Piss off
Knobface
Poowaffle

Panic! At the store

Let's play pirates!

Use the empty map below to track your quickest and most efficient way around town OR a specific shop. Arming yourself with a map and a specific list can help calm an overreactive or easily overwhelmed mind.

I bloody hate shopping!

Map your way around the store here.

Proud as punch

Pride can be hard to feel in the midst of adulthood's crazy expectations.

But hey, you're allowed to feel it, for the big stuff **AND** the small stuff.

That shit is exhausting with a messy mind so make sure to be proud of you too.

Had a shower more than once this week?

I'm proud of you.

Brave banana

Apple of achievement

Kick-ass kiwi

Proud pineapple

Grateful grape

Fill this punch bowl with all your fruity achievements!

Allow yourself to feel proud – you're worthy of that.

Revisit this page and take a huge sip of your pride punch whenever you feel a bit crappy and remember how to celebrate yourself.

Help me

A lot of us could be waist-deep in a sink hole with a hungry bear fast approaching and still find it hard to utter the words **'I need help'**... Relatable?

From mental health worries to opening a jam jar, it's okay to ask for help, but how?

Add your own ideas, too.

Use other words

_____

_____

'I think I need some guidance.'

_____

_____

'How would you tackle this?'

'Could you maybe sit with me for a while?'

_____

_____

'Can you walk me through this?'

_____

_____

Text, email or write it

Getting the words out can sometimes feel impossible. Why not write a letter?

This can be super helpful if you have anxiety surrounding face to face conversations.

There are often things we wouldn't say in person that we can say in text; let's use this loophole!

Activity time:

Create a draft text message on your phone asking for mental health help to send in times of need.

For extra convenience make a few for different scenarios.

Urgh, this sucks!

What do you need help with? Write your ideas here:

Work

Friendships

Mental health

Go on, ask for help! Scribble out each one when you do.

Strong as hell

You're not subhuman.

Asking for help is not a weakness.

You are allowed to ask for help.

Helping one another can create a stronger community.

Stop being so hard on yourself.

Hey, can you help?

Think back to times when you've helped others.

Write them here:

How did you feel when they came to you for help?

Did you think less of them?

Apply this to yourself!

No, nada, nein. How to say NO!

Your boss is asking you to work late, a family member is expecting too much from you and you've been asked to babysit for the sixth time this month...

Setting boundaries and knowing your limitations are important for a clear and healthy mind.

Can I have a collective 'heck yes' for those who struggle to say no?

HECK YES!

The world won't stop turning because you say no to covering Sharon's shift this weekend... I promise.

Someone else may cover it or they may not, but either way the world will keep spinning and there's no burden that needs to be carried!

FEELING GUILTY IS OK

Guilt, like happiness, is a normal emotion.

Feeling it doesn't mean we should go back on our no. Feel the guilt, accept it for what it is (a natural response, especially when you're a chronic people pleaser) and let it go.

It doesn't have to be subtle or a roundabout way of saying no. Be assertive and know that it's okay for you to be standing your ground. Explanations aren't a necessity when guarding your mental energy.

Besides, tiptoeing around it will only drag out the inevitable. Practise saying no in your mirror to get comfortable saying it.

SAY IT, SAY IT, SAY IT!

HONOUR YOUR FEELINGS AND DECISIONS

It's hard to disappoint someone especially when you love and respect them, however it's needed from time to time in order to guard yourself and it doesn't make you an immoral person.

Sure, help out when it feels right but respect yourself when it doesn't.

HAVING A HARD TIME SAYING NO?

Write it, text it, sing it or act it out in interpretive dance but know that however you chose to do it, you're allowed to stick to it and be firm in your decision.

Start small by saying no to the Subway employee who's asked you if you want red onion for the 90th time and gradually build up to it!

Write a big 'NO' here!

How to make friends and NOT alienate people

Adult friendships are tough. Endless promises of coffee dates and meet ups with no results. From parenthood to work commitments and just not enough hours in the day, there are many reasons why our adulthood friendships may be pushed to the bottom of the pile.

OMG we must catch up!

We'll have to meet for coffee soon!

Fitness classes.

Facebook groups (search for what interests you).

Where can I make friends?
It can be hard to make friends as an adult – here are some places you might meet like-minded people:

Dating sites (you can change the settings on most to platonic).

By taking a course or class.

Reach out to a friend you haven't seen or heard from in a while. Let them know you care.

Send a fun memory over to a friend, boost both of your moods!

Relight old flames
Aim to do these simple tasks to relight current or old friendships.

Get in touch with at least one friend this week.

Try speaking to a work colleague and get to know them a little better.

Picky
You are allowed to pick and choose who has the honour of being in your life. If a friend has become toxic you are permitted to cut them loose; you are not required to keep a friendship going if it becomes detrimental to your mental health.

Let them know
Tell your friends if you're taking a break from social media or texting. This makes them aware that you're not ignoring them whilst creating awareness of your current state.

Let them know when they've upset you, hold them accountable for fucking up AND hold yourself accountable when you've upset them; friendship is a two-way street. There should be room for mistakes, growth, learning and forgiveness.

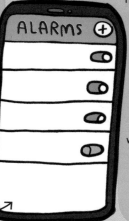

ALARMS +

Alarm bells
Set alarms in your phone to remind you to check in on friends! It's okay to forget sometimes in the whirlwind of adult life; sometimes a lil' prompt is helpful.

Who can you set alarms for? (Just try not to snooze these ones as often as your morning alarm!)

Don't be a dick

How can **YOU** make the world a little brighter?

NO, I don't mean go put on all the lights in your house... more along the lines of how you can inject some smiles and joy into the day for yourself and others?

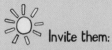 **Invite them:**

It may be a friend who says no EVERY TIME you ask them out, or a friend who has a lot of responsibility who simply can't come, but whatever the reason, make sure you continue to invite your friends out! Let them know they're still welcome.

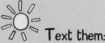 **Text them:**

Take a moment out of your day to leave a meaningful message for a friend. Let them know that they are special.

Smile away:

Smile at strangers more. Offer help to a parent struggling with a child on a noisy train. Smile and say thank you to anyone who serves you!

Be helpful:

If a colleague is in need of a shift swap and you're able to do it, a friend needs help decorating or a poorly family member needs some help with chores... do it!

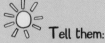 **Tell them:**

Did you notice someone doing something pretty awesome? Is a friend trying out a new hairstyle and it looks cute? Perhaps a waiter's friendliness makes you smile. Tell them! Let people know they've brightened your day and brighten theirs!

Below are some non-appearance based compliments for you to throw around like confetti. Add your own and use them freely!

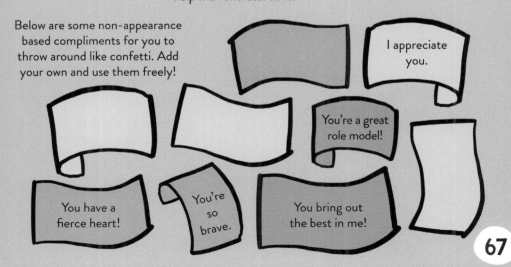

It's
okay...

Chasing life

Mark on the timeline some amazing hurdles you've reached but may not have thought to recognise previously. Here are some ideas:

Getting out of a toxic relationship.

Being self-harm free.

Leaving a job you were miserable in.

Seeking therapy.

I was born!

Honour yourself and your own expedition, put your happiness before anything else and enjoy YOUR journey.

It's okay if you're not in the same place as everyone else your age. Sure, Sue might be married in a four-bed townhouse with a dog and be jumping over all the traditional (and maybe a tad outdated) life hurdles.

However, you are not Sue.

me, now

Leave some space for future events.

It's okay not to be okay

ANGER ANNOYANCE IRRITABILITY LOW SAD CONTENT HAPPY EXCITED ECSTATIC

Did you know that all of the emotions in the scale opposite and every single one in between are perfectly normal?

Anger, annoyance and low moods are **FINE** to feel; not pleasant by any means but okay when you let them out in healthy ways.

Next time you feel anger bubbling try removing yourself from the situation and letting out the anger in a safe way.

Try screaming into a pillow. It'll help prevent uncontrollable blow outs and may enable you to resolve a situation a lot quicker!

We deserve the right to our full range of expression and emotion without shame or suppression (it'll come out one way or another so let it be without pressure).

Fill the balloon with emotions that you feel yourself suppressing and what's causing that emotion e.g. anger at someone not appreciating you.

The balloon can only hold so much before it's going to pop... see my point?

Let your emotions out in healthy ways!

Not quite the life of the party

Its 1 a.m., the music is **LOUD** and there are sweaty bodies in every inch of the room. Does that sound fun or hellish? Whatever your answer, **IT'S OKAY**.

What some may find relaxing, others may find rough.

What some may find fun, others may find fatiguing.

You get the idea. We are all wonderfully different. It's okay to be introverted, extroverted OR both AND everything in between.

What some may find exciting, others may find exhausting.

Screw this.

It's acceptable to be in your 20s and want to sit at home with Netflix and a takeaway rather than go clubbing.

Finish these sentences:

It's okay if I don't want to...

It's okay if I'd rather...

It's okay if I need to...

I don't have to...

... to be fun.

Boundary boot camp

When we create boundaries, it can lead to magical results.

It's okay to make them. Boundaries can lead to strengthened connections and a happier environment! When you identify your limitations, both mentally and physically, you take away a lot of unhelpful emotions that may emerge when you overexert yourself. **Win-win!**

It's normal for boundaries to create guilt. No one wants to disappoint others, but we don't need to feel guilt-ridden about putting our own needs first. Communicate your boundaries to the people around you and let them know WHY (if you want to). By doing this you not only allow for understanding and support from others but you open up an opportunity for them to create their own boundaries too. **Yay!**

Allow yourself to disconnect from someone else's emotional issues.

Allow yourself to a night in of recuperation instead of a night out.

Help others until it starts to drain you and then allow yourself distance.

I'm not ready to have sex. Here are my limits of how far I want to go tonight...

Ask for alone time in relationships.

Boundaries are like a wall of security; they allow us to create a safe and comforting space.

Let's build a wall! There's a door in place so we can come in and out as we please; it's important to remember that boundaries do not confine us!

Boundaries aren't about keeping you captive, they can set you free!

Write on the bricks some boundaries you are going to set and stick to!

Self-care isn't selfish

Self-care isn't always bubble baths and facemasks, sometimes it's saying no to overtime or crawling into bed at 7 p.m.

Anything that improves your wellbeing and health is self-care and it is NOT selfish. I'll say it again... putting your welfare first is NOT selfish. Got it? Great.

Add your own ideas to the lists below and start taking care of YOU!

Self-care for yo' body

Stretching

Gentle exercise

Massage

Pamper night

Visiting a doctor

Resting when poorly

Resting when you're not poorly

Self-care for yo' mind

Meditation

Use this journal (but of course I'd say that)

Sleep or switch off

Spend some quality time with a friend

See a counsellor or therapist

Self-care for yo' emotions

Get yourself out of a toxic relationship

Have a good cry

Cut ties with negative forces

I'm proud of you if you manage even one of these on a blue day.

Basic self-care tasks for when your mind says no

Brush your teeth

Put on new underwear

Eat

Hydrate

Text someone

Sometimes self-care is this.

Hey, I'm really not ok.

Life hack time

(do the cool kids still say that?)

In our low days, our hard times and our periods of pure adulting exhaustion, it can be hard to even think of self-care, let alone practise it.

It's a splendid idea, if I do say so myself, to get together a box of essentials to aid you when self-care is too much to handle.

Here are some ideas of what to pop in:

- Chewing gum
- Wet wipes
- Face wipes
- Dry shampoo
- High energy snacks, for example protein bars

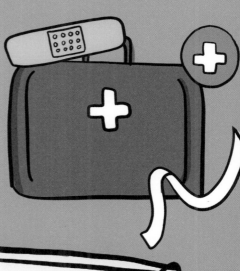

What would be in your emergency self-care box?

Draw or write the items in the box below, get it collected and have peace of mind!

Let. It. Go.

Letting go can be daunting but fear shouldn't be a reason for us to deny ourselves emotional and mental freedom; how else can we make space for amazing new memories?

Once something has completed its part in your story you are allowed to let go and free yourself of it.

It's okay to let go of resentment. You're only hurting yourself more by clinging to it.

It's okay to let go of grief. The length and breadth of your grief is not correlated to how much you loved and cared for the person or thing that you've lost.

It's okay to let go of hard feelings. We need more forgiveness in the world.

It's okay to let go of bad memories. Free yourself.

It's okay to let go of a relationship. People change, we change and that's okay.

Write what you want to be able to let go of in the balloons. Visualise them floating away from you!

Social media

Insta toxic to insta happy

Unlike the silly juice cleanses that do nothing, a social media cleanse can actually work (and you don't have to guzzle ghastly green crap).

So how do you detox your social media? Drink a load of these:

Cleanse who you follow regularly. Make sure the people you're following are enhancing or enriching your life in a positive and nourishing way.

Block accounts that you might be revisiting for negative comparisons or memories.

Use social media however and whenever you want. Screw the rules and expectations; let it serve you, you don't serve it!

No one's life is how social media portrays it. It's a highlight reel of the full movie, remember?

Social media is NOT a necessity. If it's proving too toxic or draining you are allowed to get rid of it (even if just temporarily).

Social platform
Facebook

Ways to cleanse

Question/ think about the repercussion of each status before I post it

Ahhh, a tranquil and peaceful place; your social media could be the same. Add the social media platforms you use and ways you could cleanse it or how you're going to improve your relationship with it.

Stranger danger

Children are being educated about online safety at school, but what about us adults? Everyone is at risk online if appropriate caution is not used.

STOP what you're doing and make sure **ALL** your social media accounts have two-factor authentication on. Found under your privacy settings this nifty option gives you extra security against hacking.

← double the protection

Hey, I'm meeting the guy I've been talking to online; I'm going to the pizza place near us at 6 p.m., I'll check in at regular intervals <3

Guard yourself. Online friendships can be just as meaningful as real-life ones, however we all know that it's very easy to hide a true identity behind a computer screen. Keep your common sense about you: video chat so you know who you're chatting with. If you want to meet up take someone with you for safety and meet in a busy social area.

→ Don't give out personal information such as your address.

Did you know: you can report suspicious emails to the company or website they came from.

Either get in touch via their website or via verified social media accounts to check the validity!

Scam emails can be extremely convincing... some are cringe and blatantly fake, but others are not so easy to catch out. Be cautious and never give your bank/personal details out (always try and get these things verified in two forms e.g. writing or phone) and avoid clicking on links you weren't expecting to receive.

Friend or foe

Want to know a really cool secret that might just save you a lot of issues?

You can be friends with someone in real life without being friends with them online. Mind-blowing, right?

Suzie might be the most incredible friend in person, she might be wonderful in every way BUT she might also share things online that trigger you.

I'm not saying the solution is to engage in a blocking frenzy showing no mercy, so what gentle ways can you use to make this separation?

- Facebook allows you to unfollow people without them knowing, keeping them as a friend but hiding their posts from your daily feed. This can be reversed at any point too!

- Speak to your friends before you make an action if possible. Tell them why you find their social media posts upsetting. Maybe you can resolve the issue before needing to unfriend them online.

- If you are triggered or upset every time you log into social media then the issue may lie with you. Try removing yourself from the online world for a little while, regroup and check in with your mind.

So, what's going on buddy, let it out?

I totally get it, babe.

Be gentle. It is likely your friend isn't meaning to upset or trigger you so approach the situation with love and understanding.

We've got a problem

We all know someone who's so glued to their phone that the world could be crashing down around them and they'd still be double tapping away, but when does social media actually become a problem?

Problematic behaviour is recognisable when it starts to interfere with the healthy functioning of your normal life.

Answer these questions.

Is your social media usage disturbing your productivity?
If so, pin point the times it's the most distracting.

Is checking your phone in the top five things you do in a morning?
If so, create a list below of tasks you're going to complete in a morning BEFORE you check your phone; this will help break habitual behaviours.

Is social media affecting your personal/work relationships? How?

With these answers in mind jot down some ways you can reduce your social media time.

Complete this pledge

I will aim to spend no longer than

----

on social media a day.

Signed,

You can check your usage of various apps in your phone's settings.

If you feel unable to function without social media or have a growing dependency on it then seek help; your GP can point you in the right direction.

You're worthy of a healthy mind!

Adults get bullied too

We can laugh off trolls, joke about them with our friends or just block and delete them but there's no denying that occasionally it really does sting. We're grown-ass adults so should we really be getting worked up over internet remarks? **Hell yeah**, if it's affecting you then that's valid and okay to feel whatever your age or maturity!

The truth is that adults can experience bullying in many forms and graduating our teenage years doesn't render us immune from potential online harassment. So how can we safeguard ourselves?

Harassment and abuse are harassment and abuse whether it's in the street or in your DMs. It's a crime! If you are feeling threatened, unsafe or believe you are being stalked online this should be reported to your local police department, there are special divisions dedicated to this and they are there to support you and keep you protected.

Hello, I don't feel safe online... she won't leave me alone.

If you feel you are in immediate danger call 999.

Tell somebody if you are experiencing bullying.

Don't suffer alone.

If you are being negatively affected by bullying comments or it's all getting too much, then confide and share it. A problem shared is a problem halved and the perspective of another can quell irrational thoughts.

I'm sure you would do the same for your friends, am I right?

Remove yourself from any situation that is distressing you.

You are not required to be involved. There isn't a comment thread out there that's worth putting your mental health on the line for, trust me.

See someone being bullied online?

Reach out to them and offer support and guidance.

Worried about worrying about worries

Money, money, money

It's no secret, money worries can be truly shit.

Most of us have them yet very few of us talk about them!

Worries about money can create unease, low moods, avoidance tactics and even suicidal thoughts. The pressure on men to be the only 'breadwinner' is outdated and highly patriarchal so let's raise a middle finger to gender roles and shame regarding money, you with me?

Visit Citizen's Advice and search for 'debt and money'.

We covered earlier how asking for help is okay; that extends to money worries too. You're allowed to seek education and advice with budgeting. You are also allowed to seek government help or funding if you qualify.

Debt can cause terrible stress and dealing with it alone will only add to that stress. If you feel overwhelmed and beyond your means speak with a trusted friend or visit a local Citizens Advice in your area or online.

Debt can amass for many reasons including mental health or lack of money education. There's no shame in reaching out for guidance and it might just ease your mind a little.

Do you have an open conversation with your partner/friends/family about money?

YES ☐
NO ☐

Remember, open conversations help a lot with worry. Pencil a time in your diary to have a money talk.

It's ultimately up to you how you spend your money. Jot down your incomings and outgoings together in the table, and figure out if you are living within your budget. You could even set up a spending sheet on your phone or computer to help you track spending on the go. Microsoft Excel is useful for this and countless apps are available now!

Monthly budget	
Monthly income:	+ £
Monthly bills/food:	- £
Other outgoings e.g. night's out	
Total	£

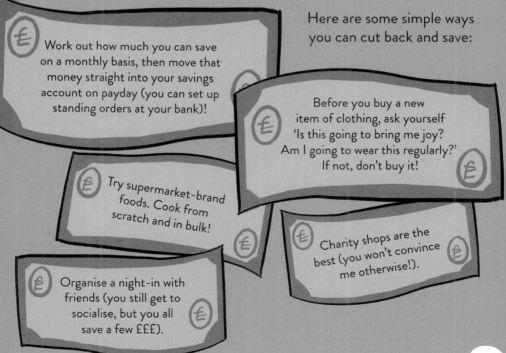

Here are some simple ways you can cut back and save:

Work out how much you can save on a monthly basis, then move that money straight into your savings account on payday (you can set up standing orders at your bank)!

Before you buy a new item of clothing, ask yourself 'Is this going to bring me joy? Am I going to wear this regularly?' If not, don't buy it!

Try supermarket-brand foods. Cook from scratch and in bulk!

Charity shops are the best (you won't convince me otherwise!).

Organise a night-in with friends (you still get to socialise, but you all save a few £££).

We communicate, we communicate not

Use these pretty petals to jot down any worries you're having about the relationships in your life, whether they're with friends, family, colleagues, partners or anyone else.

I'm worried we are drifting apart.

Communication is ALWAYS a two-way street.

How many of these worries have you communicated? If you haven't had a chat with the person, it's common for an anxious and scrambled mind to assume the worst, consequently triggering avoidance.

A healthy relationship considers uncertainties from all sides and allows for productive and respectful conversations.

So, get yapping and initiating discussions.

Worry box

Biting nails, shaking legs and tantrums are all ways in which children let us know they're feeling mega worried.

How are you communicating your worries?
(Adult tantrums in supermarket aisles aren't quite as socially accepted).

Adult life is **FILLED** with worry and it's okay to feel it!

List some of your day-to-day worries below.

Pick a phrase to help you express your worries to colleagues, friends or anyone you want to share them with.

I'm not feeling great about...

I'm overthinking this, can we talk?

I think I need your support.

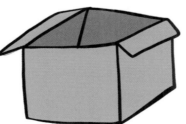

I just can't seem to stop playing it over and over.

I'm so nervous about it, can we go through it?

I'm worried, I can't rationalise it.

Can I do anything about it?

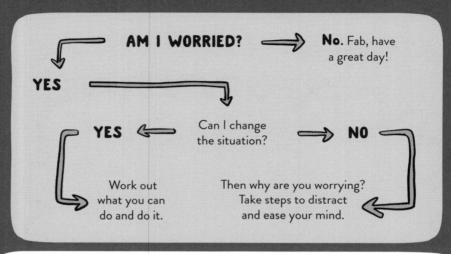

AM I WORRIED? ➡️ **No.** Fab, have a great day!

YES

Can I change the situation?

YES ⬅️ ➡️ **NO**

Work out what you can do and do it.

Then why are you worrying? Take steps to distract and ease your mind.

I like to ask myself these two simple questions when it comes to worry.

Think of a worry you currently have and apply the questions below to it.

Can I change the thing I'm worried about?

Can I do anything to ease the worry?

If you simply cannot change the situation, then worry will only force you to feel and live it again and again. Worrying about something that will inevitably happen is a complete waste of your precious brain space!

If you CAN change it then try taking small, achievable steps to do so.

Coming from a huge worry guts this all sounds very 'IT'S SO EASY, JUST STOP WORRYING!' It's not easy peasy lemon squeezy but acknowledging that worry is getting you nowhere is a step forward to changing it.

Scribble

Worry is exhausting, get it out. Use this page to wreak some havoc. Scribble on it, cry on it, write swear words on it, throw it (okay maybe don't throw it but you get the idea).

Use the trash cans to dump some of today's worries!

Let's talk about sex

No shame in the sex game

Sex and sexuality are **NOT** shameful! You are worthy and deserving of pleasure. Indulge in masturbation; take yourself to the places you want to be OR enjoy exploring all the different areas of a healthy sexual partnership!

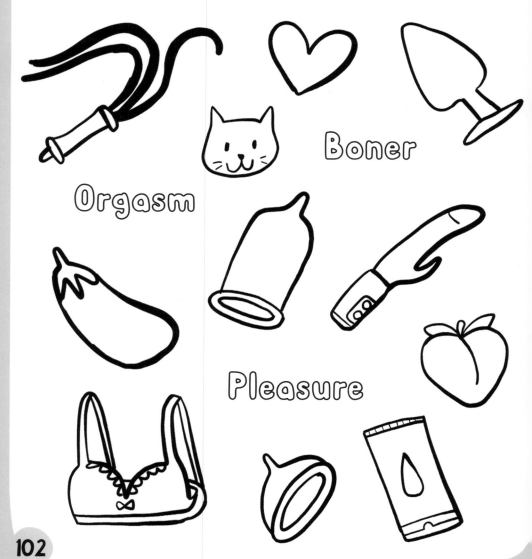

Boner

Orgasm

Pleasure

My sexuality, my choice

NO ONE has the right to humiliate you for your sexual preference OR your consensual kinks. You deserve a life lived as your true self. Anyone who won't accept that isn't worthy to be a part of your glorious existence.

Go out there and rock this world as you are.

Use this page to honour every thought and emotion you have about sex, write down your interests, your kinks, your sexual orientation and scribble down the things you might not have ever told anyone.

Be **brutally** honest with yourself! ←

Sex ed

You can see them now... that kid in secondary school who claimed to know everything about sex. What did they actually know? Not much.

Sex education in schools, especially when it comes to pleasure, is lacking, so we're left to fumble through our first sexual encounters (shall we cringe together?), learning as we go and reaching adulthood with questionable knowledge that we're still not sure is right.

I thought I'd help you out... here are some burning (sometimes literally) questions about sex with answers!

Am I supposed to orgasm every time?

Any gender should know that it's not required of you to orgasm with every sexual encounter, so take away the pressure! You can still enjoy it. Speak to your sexual partner and find out what's normal for you. Many people with vaginas can't orgasm through penetration alone.

How can I avoid UTIs?

For those with vaginas, listen up. PEE after sex. It might ruin the moment ever so slightly, but it's worth it for the avoidance of a week in hell (cystitis is truly the devil's work). Also, keep on top of personal hygiene but never put harsh soaps or products near or in your vagina.

I make your pee burn.

Should my vagina smell like...?

Rihanna had us all feeling some kind of way when she sang about liking the smell of sex. Truth is, vaginas have many odours and most of them are perfectly normal. Your sexual partner should not be expecting a waft of roses and you shouldn't either. Smells are natural and sometimes enticing! Figure out what is normal for you. If you start noticing a particularly pungent or different smell or texture then book a check up with your GP.

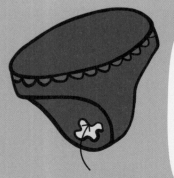

This is hella normal.

I want to try ... how do I ask my partner(s)?

It's completely normal to want to explore sexually. Always approach a sexual partner to try something new beforehand (don't drop it on them mid-sex as this can be pressuring), keep it to the point and be open. Respecting their answer is an absolute necessity. If you're feeling shy perhaps approach it in a message.

Is my penis too small?

NO. It's yours so it's perfectly fine and normal for you. Yay! Sex is pleasurable for many different reasons and whilst some may enjoy the feeling of a larger penis, some don't, and even so it doesn't mean yours is too small. Focus on connection, listening to your partner and heightening each other's senses. Try different positions, communicate and enjoy. You're perfect as you are!

Is it normal to fart during sex?

Yep... yes... sure is. Squishing yourself around like a yoga pro and exerting yourself with more vigour than a marathon runner is going to build up some gas. Farts are always funny, if one slips out then either ignore it or laugh and get back into it! Don't be ashamed of bodily functions.

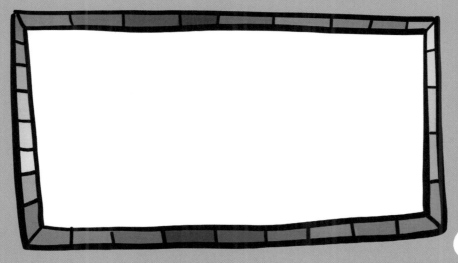

Write down some questions here that you're dying to know about sex.

Start a convo with your friends or sexual partner(s) and you'll soon see everyone has similar hang ups, and that they are normal! A little communication goes a long way.

Consent is crucial

When it comes to consent there is no room for jokes or humour. No means **NO**.

It is just as important to understand and learn how to ask for consent as it is to give it. So, let's go:

Trigger warning:

Mention of rape.

REQUIREMENTS OF CONSENT:

Your partner is freely and enthusiastically participating.

If someone is intoxicated via drink or drugs and cannot make decisions, then they cannot give consent.

Capacity to give consent can depend on learning disabilities and mental health; can the person make clear decisions and communicate them with the understanding of consequence?

Consent can be withdrawn at ANY time, including during sex. **At any time and any point.**

Persuading, pressuring or tricking someone into consent is not consent.

An unconscious person cannot give consent.

Absence of the word 'no' is not consent. Notice body language and other verbal cues.

Throughout the whole sexual encounter, you should be checking in with your sexual partner and asking if they're okay or comfortable and noticing their body language. If you go to try a new sexual activity it is crucial to also gain consent for this.

SEX WITHOUT CONSENT IS RAPE.

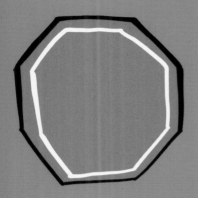

If you have been raped or sexually assaulted, please remember these things; **YOU** are **NOT** to blame in any way. Whatever your gender or age, your pain and attack is valid of reporting and you are worthy of help.

Go somewhere safe, preferably with a trusted person.

Remind yourself throughout that this is not your fault. You are not to blame. You are a victim. If you don't feel able to go to law enforcement, then confide in a loved one first, they can then help you in the next steps.

Understand that you are allowed to ask for a male or female police officer – whatever comforts you most and if at any time it is emotionally too much you are allowed to request breaks, help and support.

A forensic exam may be required. You are allowed to ask for as much information regarding this as you need. You are entitled to support and control throughout. Remember, although this process can be horrible it is ultimately there to help.

You may be advised to take emergency contraceptive and undergo an STI test. These are both for your safety. Taking along a loved one for support may help ease some anxiety.

Support and guidance for the aftermath is highly recommended, if not crucial in helping you recover from your attack. You deserve help. Don't suffer alone. You are worthy of support.

Speaking with someone impartial or unknown may help. Ask your GP to guide you in the direction of appropriate counselling.

Don't hate, masturbate

You don't need another body to be able to enjoy yourself sexually, in fact self-exploration can be incredibly empowering and liberating! Masturbation can be a way to learn what you enjoy and what you don't, it can release stress and send good feeling chemicals to your brain. We don't really ever get taught HOW to masturbate... until now:

If you have a penis:

Set the mood, get into a safe and comforting environment!

Get yourself feeling good by exploring other erogenous areas e.g. lips, neck, chest; do what feels good and notice every sensation.

TIP

Visual stimuli are great; try using erotic literature, sext with a partner or enjoy ethically sourced porn e.g. porn you have paid for.

SHAFT

Use some tactical testicle touching and explore areas around the penis, it's not just the shaft that feels good.

Your prostate can be an amazing pleasure spot! Insert a finger into your anus gently and feel around for what feels good. If you don't fancy using a finger, invest in a sex toy!

SCROTUM

Incorporate toys if you fancy it, such as a fleshlight or a vibrating ring.

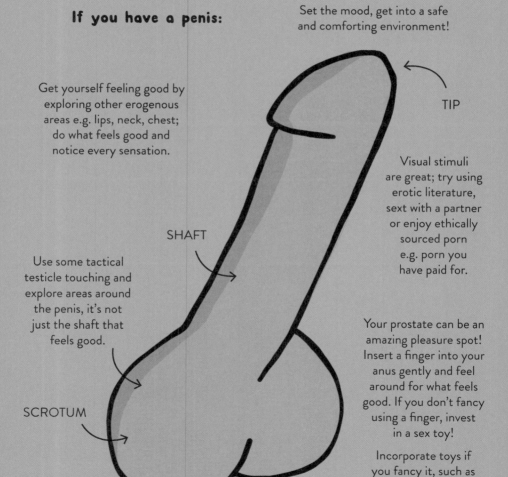

If you have a vagina:

Play, stroke and tickle parts of your body to figure out what feels good and gets you tingling (nipples, neck, stomach and legs are great places to start). A bullet vibrator is great for beginners but not essential!

Get into a comfy position, a great way to start off is on your back with legs spread out in a butterfly position.

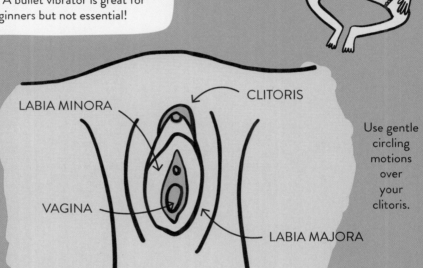

CLITORIS

LABIA MINORA

VAGINA

LABIA MAJORA

ANUS

Use gentle circling motions over your clitoris.

Insert one finger first and gently feel around for what feels good, try finger insertion whilst stimulating your clitoris with your thumb!

Visual stimuli can be a great tool, such as ethical porn or consensual images of a partner.

Some people with vaginas don't always reach orgasm every time they masturbate and that's okay!

Remember: masturbation is normal and healthy; express and explore yourself in whatever way you choose. You are worthy of pleasure!

109

Mindfulness

Calm after the storm

The mind can feel like a blustering storm; every day stresses and thoughts can whirl around like a hurricane. Write down some distressing things and worries that storm into your mind on a regular basis. Add as many or as few as you like.

Worry weather

Stressful storm

That's a lot of thoughts!

Get them stresses out!

What gentle and thoughtful ways can you minimise the stress or worry in your life? Use your stormy page as a reference.

Phew, it's a bit calmer over here!

And breathe

Calm cloud

Mindful movement

Perhaps getting off the busy bus early and walking the rest of the way or eating your lunch outside!

Meditate the haters away

When we think of meditation, we think it's hours of silent 'omm-ing' with incense burning, right? Whilst that is a super form of meditation, there are plenty more ways that fit into a busy adult life a little easier and flow with a messy mind a little smoother!

Take five minutes whilst sat at your work desk: pop on some noise cancelling headphones and play some relaxing music. Clear your mind and breathe, you can even do this in the toilet cubicle if it's not possible at your work desk!

Set an alarm for the same time each day. When the alarm goes off, check in with your body, observe which parts of your body are tense and slowly relax them. Let the tension flow out and breathe deeply.

If you don't find it easy to let your mind relax and switch off, then let someone else help. Try guided meditations.

Feeling anxious or overwhelmed? Focus on your breathing. Inhale the anxiety and exhale it out. Visualise it floating away from you, like a balloon.

Practise simple yoga poses whilst still in bed, like these:

Meditation can help create a more peaceful and healthy state of mind when life is far from peaceful or quiet. Use your short meditation times as a way to have a tiny holiday from your busy day!

Below, make a note of some times throughout the day that you could dedicate to five minutes of peaceful meditation.

- On my commute
- Before breakfast
- In the shower

Here's a breathing meditation you can try right now!

Trace your finger slowly around the circle for one full rotation as you inhale and again as you exhale. Try to trace around slower each time, practise this for five minutes each day. If you ever need calming, simply trace a circle on your desk, your leg or wherever you want and breathe.

Just breathe

116

117

Notice me, please!

There's wonder and beauty all around us just pleading to be noticed.

How many times on your commute to work or on a walk to the shop have you overlooked everything other than your phone or your worn-out trainers?

Mental health permitting, try and be a little more aware on your travels this week. Check your senses: touch, sight, taste, hearing.

What new smells have you noticed?

Some might **not** be so pleasant!

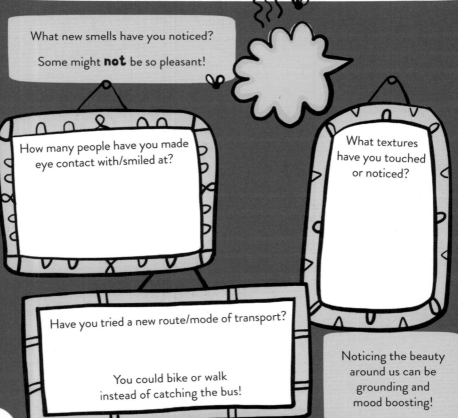

How many people have you made eye contact with/smiled at?

What textures have you touched or noticed?

Have you tried a new route/mode of transport?

You could bike or walk instead of catching the bus!

Noticing the beauty around us can be grounding and mood boosting!

Draw or write down the magical things you've noticed. Add to this page as and when you like!

This is a great way to remind yourself of all the beautiful things we miss out on by not paying attention!

Things I've noticed:

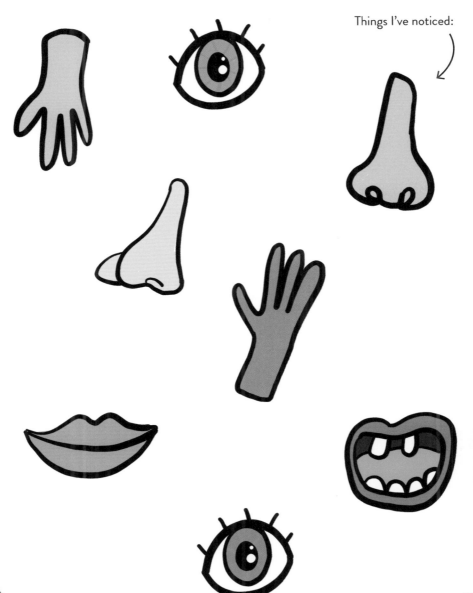

119

Self-worth, self-love, self-acceptance

Woah, you're awesome

This might be trickier than it should be (I hope it's not). I want you to FILL these pages with things that are super-awesome and amazing about yourself or even the things you just accept – you know, the shit you don't hate.

Draw, write and express yourself!

You're pretty rad

Woah, you're loyal AF

you badass

YOU GOT DIS

Revisit this page and fill it, take your time.

Would you kiss your mother with that mouth?

Write down some negative things you say to yourself, let them get woke (get it? No? Okay, I'll leave), pass them through the coffee cup of change then write a much kinder version that you could be saying on the other side!

Negative self-talk

I'm so useless, I always get things wrong.

An example is already in to get you started.

The way you speak to yourself **MATTERS!**
If talking kindly to houseplants can help
them flourish, then IMAGINE
what it can do for you!

Everything is better with
a morning coffee. So, let's
caffeinate some of the negative
self-talk we have and make
them a little brighter!

Kind self-talk

I'm always trying and putting myself out
there, I rise to a challenge.

CUP
OF
CHANGE

Stop, right now

We can all be master self-saboteurs when we want to be. Stop hindering your own journey!

Here are some things we need to STOP doing. Some of the signs are left blank for you to add your own!

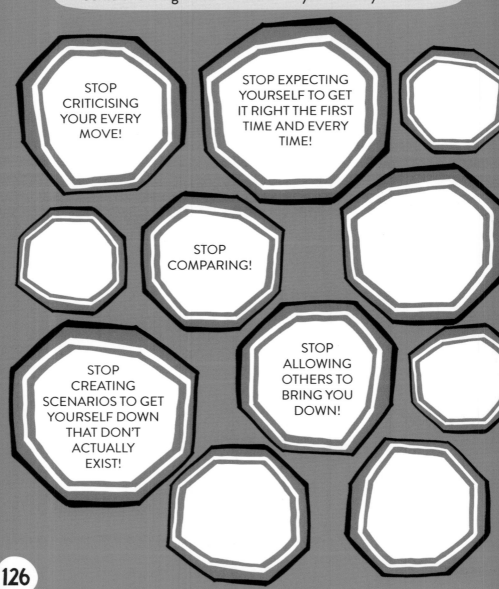

STOP CRITICISING YOUR EVERY MOVE!

STOP EXPECTING YOURSELF TO GET IT RIGHT THE FIRST TIME AND EVERY TIME!

STOP COMPARING!

STOP CREATING SCENARIOS TO GET YOURSELF DOWN THAT DON'T ACTUALLY EXIST!

STOP ALLOWING OTHERS TO BRING YOU DOWN!

R-E-S-P-E-C-T

Not giving yourself a proper lunch break, working over dedicated self-care time, being cruel to yourself... these are just a few of the many ways that we can disrespect ourselves. It's going to happen every now and again and it's okay!

Here's an award for being the incredible human that you are.

Write yourself a little speech to thank yourself for all the times you HAVE shown yourself respect, how you're going to respect yourself in the future and a vow to try and minimise the times of disrespect.

I'll get the tissues ready.

You're magic

Well, we've been on quite a journey together.
Thank you for taking it with me and I hope
you've learnt something that might just
make adult life a little easier.

I would like to leave you with this
message, which applies to each
and EVERY one of you.

No exceptions, no ifs and no buts.

Thank you for being here.

All my love,
Milly X

What have you gained from
your Adulting Manual?

I was kind to myself

Life is hard!

I went to my appointment

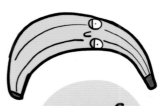

I went outside today

I DID IT!

I WAS BRAVE TODAY

IN AN
EMERGENCY

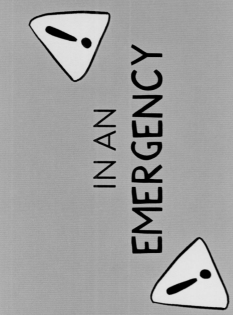

IN AN
EMERGENCY

IN AN
EMERGENCY

IN AN
EMERGENCY

My warning signs of a low mood are:

_____
_____

If I start to feel low, I can distract myself by:

_____
_____

If my distractions don't work, I can call/ text:

_____
_____

If they don't answer I can use a local crisis line which is:

_____
_____

If I have an urge to hurt myself, I can go here to keep myself safe:

_____
_____

My warning signs of a low mood are:

_____
_____

If I start to feel low, I can distract myself by:

_____
_____

If my distractions don't work, I can call/ text:

_____
_____

If they don't answer I can use a local crisis line which is:

_____
_____

If I have an urge to hurt myself, I can go here to keep myself safe:

_____
_____

My warning signs of a low mood are:

_____
_____

If I start to feel low, I can distract myself by:

_____
_____

If my distractions don't work, I can call/ text:

_____
_____

If they don't answer I can use a local crisis line which is:

_____
_____

If I have an urge to hurt myself, I can go here to keep myself safe:

_____
_____

My warning signs of a low mood are:

_____
_____

If I start to feel low, I can distract myself by:

_____
_____

If my distractions don't work, I can call/ text:

_____
_____

If they don't answer I can use a local crisis line which is:

_____
_____

If I have an urge to hurt myself, I can go here to keep myself safe:

_____
_____

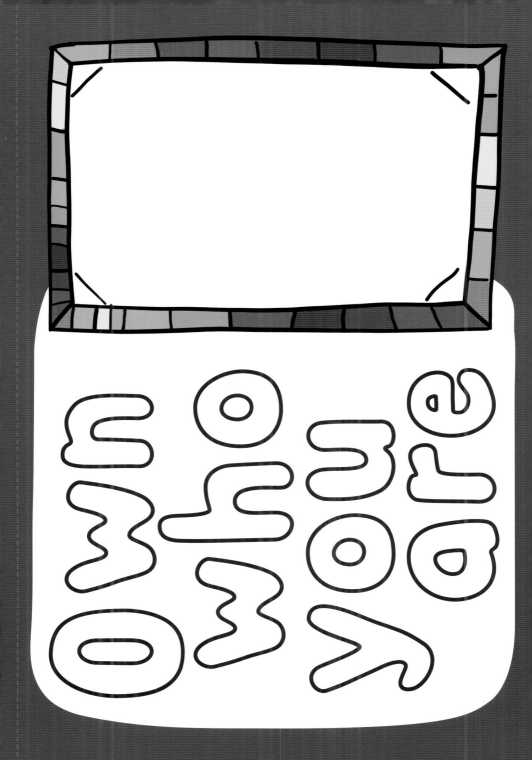

own who you are

Badass SURVIVOR

Write a lovely note to yourself, pop it in your 'crisis box' or stick
it in the bottom of a drawer for you to discover another time!